Open the

Ayşe Meliz

Open the Light © 2023 Ayşe Meliz

All rights reserved.

No part of this publication may be reproduced, stored in a retrieval system, or transmitted, in any form or by any means, electronic, mechanical, photocopying, recording or otherwise, without the prior written permission of the presenters.

Ayşe Meliz asserts the moral right to be identified as author of this work.

Presentation by *BookLeaf Publishing*

Web: www.bookleafpub.com

E-mail: info@bookleafpub.com

ISBN: 9789357740012

First edition 2023

These poems are dedicated to all those whose light shines so bright that you light up others from within. To the ones who bring the light, are the light, held the light. They're for those for whom the darkness has become a friend. For those controlling life on a dimmer switch, trying to get it just right.

These poems are for you.

ACKNOWLEDGEMENT

This book quite literally wouldn't have been possible if it wasn't for my dear friend, V- and our phones, who are always listening.

Ongoing and everlasting thanks to my family, without whom, not only would I not be here, but I wouldn't be me. Your love and support is everything.

Little Z, for always have two ears to listen to me with and and for being my third and fourth eye.

And to Bob, for those early days.

When I count my blessings, I count you all twice.

PREFACE

It was a cold January night when at a belated Christmas catch up, I sat chatting with a very dear friend. I shared my dreams of publishing a book someday and low and behold, the next day, my feeds were full of adverts for TheWriteAngle writing challenge.

Writing this collection of poetry has been a cathartic and energising process and one I wish I'd started much sooner.

Dear Reader, I hope you enjoy them and that they add something to the rich tapestry of your own life.

Sliced Bread

Do you know what it's like
to have your own personal cheerleader
Backing your every move
Willing you to win
To be the best version of yourself
And then some
Do you know what it's like
to have the person that raised you
put you high on a pedestal
and then ensure that you prove to
everyone else that it's exactly where you belong
Do you know what it's like
to be surrounded by people
who genuinely believe that you are
not only the best thing since sliced bread
but that also, the sun does actually shine....
Do you know what it's like
to be loved so wholly and unconditionally
That even in your darkest moments
You had the strength to
Open the Light
To pick yourself back up again
And to fight another day
I hope you do.

The Circle

Endless and forever
Of life and the hereafter
No beginning and no end
Constant.
Like the never ending smile
of a kindly grandma
Strong and sturdy
Reliable.
I can predict its every turn
And yet I know not what comes next
But the hope of another sunrise
Lives within and keeps me going
For eternity.

Red Packets

I can't believe I'm missing this
Her big day; their union
But the possible alternative,
of missing a separation; a life from this world...
I can't.
I visit. Far too early. It might be an intrusion.
Smiles all around and a tongue
So familiar and yet still so foreign
She is of course radiant
As if she could be anything less
I choke. I stumble.
My smile painted onto my face
I can't stand the happiness
I am not a part of it, my body rejects it.
I feel the familiar pain flooding my senses
and realise, I have to leave.
In a flurry of congratulations and best wishes
I desperately seek out an exit
I need to take this pain away from here
It doesn't belong and by extension, neither do I.
Red packets, grabbed by the handful
are pushed into my hands
"They'll bring luck!" I'm told
And oh, how I wished they would!
By the next day

In a vacant room
All that's left is the bright red, lucky packet
staring back at me, a beacon of hope
Reminding me of the many things I have lost.

ID Badge

Each label, every title
Gave an identity
A sense of meaning
A purpose
A defining role
A link to the past
And something to take to the future
Officially recorded
A badge of honour
And I have worn each with pride
But one by one
As the labels have been retired
I find they have taken little parts of me with them too
Leaving me a lesser version of myself
Less sure, less confident
Left in a world with less love
And less laughs
Less secure
More curious
And sometimes brave enough
to dream of the next moniker I can adopt.

TTLC
(Turkish Tender Loving Care)

Love requires care
A delicate hand
Attention to detail
It is fragile
Built up from nothing
And even with roots that burrow deep
Dainty flowers need a gentle touch
Don't be clumsy with a blossom eyed lover
Don't try to change or interrogate
And whatever you do don't give up
Love and love hard
Remember that once, you would have seized the rays of sun for them if that's what they'd wanted.

Lost

'It is better to have loved and lost
Than never to have loved at all'
We are told
Each connection sustaining growth
Revealing more of the person you are
Lessons learned
New opportunities sought
But how many times can a heart
be cracked open, torn apart and shredded
Before there is no recovery
And you are left, full of despair
Destroyed
Vacant, yet full of the knowledge
You have lost yourself.

Ch-ch-ch-ch-ch-ch-Changes

Blossoming, developing, growing
The four seasons
The reaching of maturity
Milestones met

Death, decay, destruction
The pain of loss
The sudden passing
Lifetimes celebrated

Happiness, joy, elation
That burst of pride
A tingle down the spine
Each moment wondrous

The change will come
Of this I am sure
It is, after all
The only constant.

Less

Hopeless. We've been careless with our world
Endless is the bombardment of misery
from both near and far
A feckless way of life, driven
by a senseless greed and meaningless priorities
Culminating to leave us, rudderless
Inundated with worthless riches
Clueless to the real treasures to be found
So many dauntless or impervious
to the horrors that are around
Sleepless nights take over for
those with more than mindless thoughts
Regardless of the change they try to affect, they remain
Powerless and impotent.
Limitless drive for more
When all we're left with is less
and the pleas to be blessed
Flawless imperfection, effortless energies
and motionless drive.
Nevertheless, sure as the sun will rise
We will strive, WE will rise
for more.

Jungle Feelings

The fear runs thick
cutting deep
A canyon through the
Jungle of paradise that had been

The confusion clouds my mind
Uncertain, like a young bird
before he takes his first flight,
Weighs me down.

The anxiety coursing through
my veins, like a Class A
Reverberating around, enjoying
The party far more than me

The despair. Flat. Despondent.
Lifeless. A sense of mourning
The big cats, monkeys and elephants
Gone

Their ashes fall to the ground forming a thick
carpet
And all the colour and vibrancy that once was
The elation and hope, the very fibre of my being
Is no more.

Looking in the Mirror

I don't know her anymore.
She has more lines,
more wrinkles
She smiles less
Her light is dull
Her energy, off.
She looks like someone
I used to know
Distantly familiar
But now, she looks sad.
I want to help her,
See her face light up
See her fire ignite
See her come back to
the person I knew
See her come back, to me.

.L.I.F.E.

L is for the longevity and virility,
the abundance of love

I is for the selfish nature of the
human and its need for power and domination

F is for the freedoms denied to so many,
those poor unfortunate souls

And E. E is for the eternity
That allows for the cyclical, undulating patterns.

Life. It is, for the lucky few.

Who has been here?

There's a shade of grey
I've never seen before
Tinged with despair and grief
Settles, thicker than any dust I've known.
A coldness that bites
As harsh and as cruel
as the initial devastation. It will kill.
"Sesimi duyan var mı?"*
The chant of the rescuers, after three
Like the traveller of distant memories past
I wonder if their voices can be heard
By some poor soul, trapped
Entombed in the place once called home
What was a place of sanctuary.
No chanting, prayers or drilling now
The silence, deafening
So full of desperate hope
Has he been here?
Our prayers so callously discarded, tossed aside?
Hearts so heavy
The guilt of being spared
The shame of not being able to do more.
And then, as distant as the
memories of the life that once was
The muffled crying of a baby.

A renewed energy engulfs the masses
And before long
Without knowing if he's listening, or if he's even there
The chants exclaim of God's greatness
And with the miracle we see before us now,
Who are we to disagree?

* 'Sesimi duyan var mı?' translates from Turkish to say; 'Can anyone hear my voice?'

Journey Planner

There's been a change of plans.
I'm not sure what comes next
I'm not even really sure what's already
happened.
But there's been a change of plans.
My road map was inaccurate
Hidden obstacles as
Immovable as mountains
Complications like a diversion
from Spaghetti Junction,
Demand a new route.
There'll need to be a change of plans
That's fine, I think.
But as I begin to charter my new course
My new plan
A longer task, a longer journey
I find I no longer know
If I'm headed to the original destination.
There's been a change of plans, I hear.
And then I decide that the plan,
any plan, is redundant
And I sit back to enjoy the journey.
There's been a change of plans, you see.

Visible Scars

I am used to the scars being internal
Private. For me to see, for me to feel
Not to be shared with others
My own personal hell
The dull, repetitive thuds hurt
The pain, now external too
And as quickly as it started, it stops
Relief washes over me as I
struggle to catch my breath
The gentle, familiar hand
tucks my curls behind my ear.
Like a frightened animal
I don't know which way to turn
What to do to ensure my survival?
His words hit harder than any other blow yet
Hid disdain and cruelty
Busily burying themselves in
the crevices of my heart
that once held our love.
And,with a final strike, he's gone.
The sun shines brightly
into my eyes, out of place.
Is it safe to move?
Surely I'm not safe out in the open
As I scramble to gather

my thoughts, my belongings
and the remnants of my pride
I wonder how it's come to this.
As the door closes, I realise I am safe
But the visible scars will tell this story.

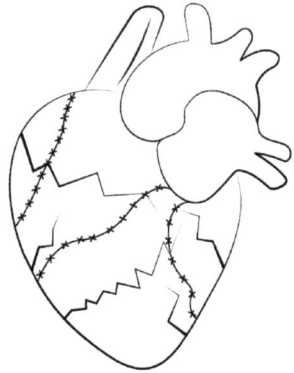

Inertia.

I want to, but I can't
I'm stuck or trapped
Or both
I need to, but I can't
The weight of several worlds
Crushing down on me
I have to, but I can't
It's too much or not enough
Or maybe neither
Will you help me?
Can you help me?
The Room is empty and I realise that
the external force, will have to be,
Me.

The Time Thief

I am so glad I have stolen
these last few moments with you
You were with me from my beginning
And I will be with you till your end
I hope you're not scared
Because I'm scared for you
Can you hear it in my voice?
I hope not, it's true.
Can I get you some water?
An ice cube, perhaps?
Do your pillows need fluffing?
What more can I do?
To show you just
How loved you are, will always be...
Do I remember the countless ways you loved
me?
Of course I do!
Could I forget them?
Not likely!
How could I forget the endless sacrifice
the generosity, the kindness
Your love has held me and fed me, challenged
me,
taught me, guided me and enveloped me
I am me because you are you

Your stories and lessons, your sayings, they're all in my head
I don't know it now but I will come to hate that I haven't written them down.
34 years to the day
And he's coming for you
Or so they say
But I'm sorry, I won't let him take you away
Oh no, not today.
It's not your time. There's still so much to do
I haven't had my fill of you
I haven't yet repaid you
Nor loved you hard enough
We haven't had just quite long enough
But as you take your last breaths,
surrounded by all those who love you
Looking a little less like you
Sounding a lot less like you
I realise, that no matter when or where you go
I shall carry you with me
Always.

The River

The river is a deep blue
And it has meandered its way through my life
Flowing through my every fibre
Like the blood through my veins
Hydro-powering me through ups and downs
Big as mountains
And those as insignificant as crumbs after a picnic.
The source of the river
A quiet corner, the gentle tweeting of birds
Always so full of brilliant sunlight and hope
A place of comfort and reflection
The river will outrun me,
Of this, I am certain
Oh how I long to find the stormy sea
into which it will flow
Washing away with it
sorrows and stories
of a distant past.

We are all Fruit (but we are not bananas).

Fruit corner sits proud; right there, in the corner
Where the two edges of the worktop meet
Well stocked in abundance and variety
We are lucky.
The humble banana, despite its cheerful appearance
Knows not of the misery it can bring the others
How, as its own life begins to fade
It will zap the joy from them
Dull their spark.

The banana only gets one shot at life
It is often well travelled and may
have seen more of the world than you or I
Some will be destined to be eaten fresh
Mushier others will be turned into loaves
Leaving the sorry few to be discarded
No longer the colour of the sun
Full of promise and hope
To fulfil their destinies

But you, you my dear
Are nothging li-li-like a banana
You have many destinies to fulfil
And multiple opportunities to succeed at them
You do not have only one shot at this life
Before you are so callously discarded

For all we know, even by the end of your life
After multiple shots and changes of plans
Like a passion fruit, despite your withered outside
You could still be full of life and zest within.

Karate Chops & Beyond

Even though I am so full of emotion
I love and accept myself just as I am

So much hurt, sorrow and shame
I fear it will beat me before I it

89 days or is it more?
Not since you left
But since I experienced the most basic
of human interactions

A simple touch,
a brush of the fingers,
a guiding hand on the back
a reassuring squeeze of the hand.

If I close my eyes tightly
And open my mind widely
I can just about summon the courage
To remember the warmth of an embrace
Being enveloped by love
Being held. Safe
Bubbles are no longer child's play
But invisible barriers. Like prisons
They keep us at bay.

Even though I know I am loved
I find my current situation hard to accept

The tapping, the repetition, the touch
It saves me
Rescues me from the hurt, sorrow and shame

I am my own Martial Arts Hero
and I have no need for a knight in shining armour,
For I shine brighter than any metal he could ever wear.

I remember

I remember this one time, dancing in the kitchen
The potatoes in the oven
Just the way I liked them
Just the way you'd make them
I remember eating at the table
I don't do that anymore
Only if it's a special occasion
I remember this one time, sitting on your bed
Our family all around us
Though it was only in your head
I remember the comfort that it brought you
And the stories that you told
I remember realising, I'd left this too late
And how now you were probably a bit too old
I remember this one time in the hospital
You didn't know I was there
I'd had this feeling I should go
Despite the state of my hair
And oh how I wish that
I'd stayed a little longer
Kept you company and held your hand
Because the next time I did it was cold and unplanned
I remember this and so much more
Because those last few weeks...
I wish…
we'd had more.

Have you ever?

Have you ever laughed so hard
You genuinely didn't know
if you'd already taken your last breath?
Have you ever laughed so hard
That you've awoken to the sight
Of the cold, hard floor?
Have you ever laughed so hard
that bright red droplets have
sprung from your nose?
If your answer is no,
then I am telling you
my friend
That you haven't really laughed at all
Haven't felt that sense of awe, tinged with fear
Haven't ached at your sides, wondering if you'd tear
If you think that Mary Poppins, both one and two
Are an exaggeration, a hyperbole
Then my friend, this one's for you
You need to go and laugh.
My laughter is most frequently teased out around
Little Z
For it really is only she
Who can make me question my own mortality,
whilst I am having
the time of my life.

Milton Keynes UK
Ingram Content Group UK Ltd.
UKHW020925241123
433194UK00017B/1202